D1483219

WILD IS
THE WIND

WILD IS THE WIND

FARRAR STRAUS GIROUX / NEW YORK

CARL PHILLIPS

Farrar, Straus and Giroux

175 Varick Street, New York 10014

Copyright © 2018 by Carl Phillips
Printed in the United States of America

First edition, 2018

Image on page xiii: Detail from *Rinaldo* by Tom Knechtel;
courtesy of Marc Selwyn Fine Art.

Library of Congress Cataloging-in-Publication Data

Names: Phillips, Carl, 1959- author.

Title: Wild is the wind : poems / Carl Phillips.

Description: First edition. | New York : Farrar, Straus and Giroux, 2018. |
Includes bibliographical references .

Identifiers: LCCN 2017025629 | ISBN 9780374290269 (hardcover) |
ISBN 9780374717100 (ebook)

Classification: LCC PS3566.H476 A6 2018 | DDC 811/.54—dc23

LC record available at https://lccn.loc.gov/2017025629

Designed by Quemadura

Our books may be purchased in bulk for promotional, educational,
or business use. Please contact your local bookseller or the Macmillan
Corporate and Premium Sales Department at 1-800-221-7945, extension
5442, or by e-mail at MacmillanSpecialMarkets@macmillan.com.

www.fsgbooks.com
www.twitter.com/fsgbooks
www.facebook.com/fsgbooks

1 3 5 7 9 10 8 6 4 2

FOR RESTON

more rough, less blue, more lit, and patternless

CONTENTS

WILD IS
THE WIND

COURTSHIP

—Both things, I think. But less the hesitation of many hands touching the stunned dethronement of the master's body, than their way of touching it again; again. Each time, more surely.

SWIMMING

Some nights, I rise from the latest excuse for
Why not stay awhile, usually that hour when
the coyotes roam the streets as if they've always
owned the place and had come back inspecting now
for damage. But what hasn't been damaged? History
here means a history of storms rushing the trees
for so long, their bowed shapes seem a kind of star—
worth trusting, I mean, as in how the helmsman,
steering home, knows what star to lean on. Do
people, anymore, even say helmsman? Everything
in waves, or at least wave-like, as when another's
suffering, being greater, displaces our own, or
I understand it should, which is meant to be
different, I'm sure of it, from that pleasure
Lucretius speaks of, in witnessing from land
a ship foundering at sea, though more and more
it all seems related. I love the nights here. I love
the jetty's black ghost-finger, how it calms
the harbor, how the fog hanging stranded just
above the water is fog, finally, not the left-behind

parts of those questions from which I half wish
I could school my mind, desperate cargo,
to keep a little distance. An old map from when
this place was first settled shows monsters
everywhere, once the shore gives out—it can still
feel like that: I dive in, and they rise like faithfulness
itself, watery pallbearers heading seaward, and
I the raft they steady. It seems there's no turning back.

BROTHERS IN ARMS

The sea was one thing, once; the field another. Either way,
something got crossed, or didn't. Who's to say, about
happiness? Whatever country, I mean, where inconceivable
was a word like any other lies far behind me now. I've
learned to spare what's failing, if it can keep what's living
alive still, maybe just
                              a while longer. Ghost bamboo that
the birds nest in, for example, not noticing the leaves, color
of surrender, color of poverty as I used to imagine it when
I myself was poor but had no idea of it. I've always thought
gratitude's the one correct response to having been made,
however painfully, to see this life more up close. *The higher
gods having long refused me, let the gods deemed lesser
do the best they can*—so a friend I somewhere along the way
lost hold of used to drunkenly announce, usually just before
passing out. I think he actually believed that stuff; he must
surely, by now, be dead. There's a rumored
                                                            humbling effect
to loss that I bear no trace of. It's not loss that humbles me.
What used to look like memory—clouds for hours breaking,

gathering, then breaking up again—lately seems instead

like a dance, one of those slower, too-complicated numbers

I never had much time for. Not knowing exactly what it's

come to is so much different from understanding that it's come

to nothing. Why is it, then, each day, they feel more the same?

MEDITATION: ON BEING
A MYSTERY TO ONESELF

The oars of the ship called *Late Forgiveness* lift,
then fall. The slaves at the oars
have done singing—it's pure work, now.
The galley master stands as always, whip in hand,
but for the moment
                    in idleness. They say when discipline
dreams, it's just the one dream: hands
breaking from stillness, like hands of course, but like
hands when, having lost a thing entirely, they move
entirely by definition. The ship
moves slowly. It's a ship. It's a storm-beclouded
stronghold
                    in the dark, receding. They say discipline's flag
is blue—three deer in flight; three stars
barely show, above them.

MUSCULATURE

The last dog I owned, or—more humanely put, so
I'm told—that I used to live with, she'd follow me
everywhere. She died eventually. I put her down's
more the truth. It *is* the truth. And now

                                    this dog—that
I mostly call Sovereignty, both for how sovereignty,
like fascination, can be overrated, and for how long it's
taken me, just to half understand that. Pretty much my
whole life. Mortality seemed an ignorable wilderness
like any other; the past seemed what, occasionally, it
still does, a version of luck when luck, as if inevitably,
gets stripped away: What hope, otherwise, for suffering?
When did honesty become so hard to step into and stay
inside of, I'm not saying

                          forever, I could last a fair time
on a small while. Sovereignty sleeps hard beside me. I
pass my hands down the full length of him, like a loose
command through a summer garden. Let those plants
that can do so lean away on their stems, toward the sun.

GIVINGLY

—So here we are again, one-handedly fingering
the puckered edges of the exit wounds
memory leaves behind, he said, and he tossed
his leash made of stars, then tightened it,

around the antlers it seems I forget, always,
about having. Smell of nightfall when it
hasn't settled yet. Insatiability and
whatever else hidden behind the parts

that hide it. Surely any victim—sacrificial
or not—deserves better, I thought, him leading me
meanwhile toward the usual place, the branches
grow more givingly apart there, as if to say

Let pass. The wind was clean. The wind
was a good thing, in his hair, and across our faces.

THE DISTANCE AND THE SPOILS

Half a life; a life . . . So much turns out to have
been neither history nor memory, that mirage
of history, in which *I want you* came at least
briefly close. Sometimes
disclosure's a pretty
flower, and that's the end of it. Say he lifted
himself slow, rose unsteadily up, sleep-or-
dream-staggered out into black of night, non-
choiring of crickets with their sounds that we
call song, fall or don't, speed—for a change—of
not falling, what became
of that? Sometimes
we want a thing more than we can admit we
want that thing. Invisible leaves toss like water;
the eyes shut, or they turn away, as from the four
bright points of a constellation missed earlier,
and just now seen clearly: pain; indifference;
torn trust; permission. Rest. Lean against me.

NOT THE WAVES AS THEY
MAKE THEIR WAY FORWARD

Like Virgil, Marcus Aurelius died believing that his triumphs,
when pitched against his failures, had come to very little.
I don't know. Given the messiness of most lives (humble,
legendary, all the rest in between)—their interiors,
I mean—it's hard to say he was wrong. Black night. Black
train. Freight of worries. Things that stay
the same. Having reached that point that even
the luckiest sometimes never get close to, where
desire at last offers nothing more—nor less—than
what restraint can, Marcus Aurelius wrote down
some thoughts meant apparently only for himself, though
they became *Meditations*, a book without which, by now,
he'd pretty much be forgotten. It begins with gratitude.
How it ends is painful, if I'm remembering right. But it isn't pain.

GOLD LEAF

To lift, without ever asking what animal exactly it once belonged to,
the socketed helmet that what's left of the skull equals
up to your face, to hold it there, mask-like, to look through it until
looking through means looking back, back through the skull,
into the self that is partly the animal you've always wanted to be,
that—depending—fear has prevented or rescued you from becoming,
to know utterly what you'll never be, to understand in doing so
what you are, and say no to it, not to who you are, to say no to despair.

SEVERAL BIRDS IN HAND
BUT THE REST GO FREE

Hiking the restored prairie was more than lovely enough—
I could appreciate the good signage; got a chance to forget,
for a change, to respect fear . . . Were they happy in any
real way, whatever real is, those first

                                        pioneers? The happiest
people I know are those whose main strategy has
always been detachment. I've been working on that. Not so
long ago, for example, a sentence like "The skin where you
burned me last week with your cigarette has almost healed
completely"

                    was so much harder to say. Progress. The way
bluestem, mallow, purple globes of clover, when said
together, make a kind of music, though they're nothing alike,
pale colors in a tall field—

                                all a prairie comes to. True pity,
as in deeply felt—I save mine, what's left of it, for
the wounded animals, the ones not yet dead. Already I don't
mean, anymore, the soft dark violent rustling wilderness
inside the bright one that I was before, when I say wilderness.

STRAY

When he speaks of deserved and undeserved as more
than terms—how they can matter, suddenly—I can tell
he believes it. Sometimes a thing can seem star-like
when it's just a star, stripped of whatever small form of joy
likeness equals. Sometimes the thought that I'm doomed
to fail—that the body is—keeps me almost steady, if
steadiness is what a gift for a while brings—feathers, burst-
at-last pods of milkweed, October—before it all fades away.
Before the drugs and the loud music, before tears and
restraining orders and the eventual *Go fuck yourself get your
ass out of here don't go*, the apartments across the street
were a boys' grammar school—before that, a convent,
the only remains of which, ornamenting the far parking lot,
is a marble pedestal with some Latin on it that translates as
"Heart of Jesus, have mercy," as if that much, at least, still
remained relevant, or should. If it's true that secrets resist
always the act of telling, how come secrets, more often than
not, seem the entire story? Caladium, cleome—how delicate,
this holding of certain words in the mouth, the all-but-lost
trick of lifting for salvage the last windfalls as, across them,
the bees make their slow-muscled, stunned, moving scab . . .

REVOLVER

His face was a festival. Inside it,
as if helplessness remained
one of the few things left worth
fretting for, making some kind of
show of, whatever lies
half between, he turned,
kept turning . . . Above him, leaves
swam the air—so it couldn't have been
past November. Most animals, smelling
death on another, back away,
as if repulsed, or frightened; the rest
come closer. It was
like that, then less so. His face
was a festival, within which—just as
tenderness is only sometimes
weakness, or how what we were
can become unrecognizable to what we are,
or think we are—leaves swam the air.

THE DARK NO SOFTER
THAN IT WAS BEFORE

How I say it happened
may not be how it happened. In that slum
that the mind lately feels like, I'm walking as if
forever toward where the chestnut trees flanking
the brokenly lit boulevard—what's
left of it—come now to a point, now
to the never-to-be-reached conclusion I suspect
they've meant all along. It's a slum, but the sea
hugs it as it does so many places prettier, emptier
of such distractions as fear and at least the more
galvanizing varieties of sorrow, hence the not-so-muffled
crashing of waves not far from here: *blue dart,*
shattered crossbow . . . Keeping it all somehow differently alive,
and close, that's the point, someone told me once—
who? and the point of what? The less I understand myself,
the more I understand others, which I used to think wasn't
saying much, but there are nights it can seem as good a road as any
maybe toward compassion, even if half
washed away—the road, I mean; not compassion. I don't know
how the better parts between two people become the first forgotten.

FROM A BONFIRE

There's plenty I miss, still, that I wouldn't want back—
which I'm beginning to think might be all regret's ever had
to mean, and there's maybe no shame, then, in having
known some and, all these years, I've pretty much
been wrong. Not that being wrong means wasting time,
exactly. What hasn't been useful? Having grown up with
bonfires each October, having equated them with fall,
the communion especially of leaves falling, fire as
what both defined the dark—easily taken for granted—
and kept the dark at bay, surely that's been worth
something, for it stays with me; in that way, it even now
marks a difference between who I was and what I've
since become: a kind of bonfire myself—unattached,
though, to any time of year in particular, instead
a season of the mind entirely, as unpredictable
in occurrence as in intensity, cracked, blue,
forever half done departing, not so different
after all, maybe, from the darkness against which
I'm at once more apparent and somehow more
betrayed. *What has restlessness been for*, the darkness

asks, as if that were the question, when the darkness
itself is its own question, the most honest one left,
as far as I can see, that's worth asking, that I keep
meaning to ask, then faltering, not at all out of fear,
I think—I don't think I'm afraid—but being fire, and restless.

AND LOVE YOU TOO

When he describes a spear passing
through the throat of some otherwise
bronze-protected warrior, part of what Homer
means is death, and there's a piece that isn't,
the way black can resemble more a brightness
sometimes, or how wind can vacillate
between being a force bearing down
on a field and what, for a time at least, from
beneath, gives

              or seems to give to the field
some agency ... For the gods in Homer, there's an
at once lovely and less-than-lovely
patterning to the brutality that, even as
they wield it, is only theirs to borrow; Fate
stakes the final claim, as if forever breaking
ground for an imagined city from which
the idea is that a vast empire like a fist opening
fans out

              eventually across all things divine
and mortal. Just as softly as the face,

when the body's sleeping, returns to childhood,
Closer, deeper, says the hole in history
we call the mouth of Homer because it
helps, to name. Not the song that fog-muffled
bells make, after storm. Nothing winged and lost,
rising. Blood's what the wound keeps gushing.

WHAT I SEE IS THE LIGHT
FALLING ALL AROUND US

To have understood some small piece of the world
more deeply doesn't have to mean we're not as lost
as before, or so it seems this morning, random bees
stirring among the dogwood blossoms, a few here
and there stirring differently somehow, more like
resisting stillness . . . Should it come to winnowing
my addictions, I'd hold on hardest, I'm pretty sure,
to mystery, though just yesterday, a perfect stranger
was so insistent that I looked familiar, it seemed
easier in the end to agree we must know each other.
To his body, a muscularity both at odds and at one
with how fragile everything else about him, I thought,
would be, if I could see inside. What's the word
for the kind of loneliness that can feel like swimming
unassisted in a foreign language, for the very first time?

BLACK AND COPPER IN

A CRUSH OF FLOWERS

Weapons thrown aside, despite
duty; smell of sorrow recalling mostly the sea,
even many years inland; lions devouring, right in
front of you, your best horse: everything's
somebody's history. *Once, beside a windbreak of pines*
and holly trees, I was told to forget having heard
what I was pretty sure
I'd just heard, he said, looking
through a window in whose reflection I carefully
watched myself undressing, not being looked at, and
not minding especially, though *Yeah and meanwhile*
all of it amounting to what now exactly, mister, I
wanted to say, but—
who says that? Rampant: that's
what they call a lion when shown standing on its hind
legs in heraldry, heraldry as in symbols like crowns,
double roses, severed hands with lace cuffs arranged
so, across a breastplate, a shield, letterhead, affection

born from a pride that's, by now,

also history. Who can

say what's true in the end? Other than the flexed

claws of it, extending outward from inside the body—

and those parts, accordingly, where indifference flourishes

going hushed, a moment—I hardly know what

the truth's for, really. If I'm frightened, shouldn't I be.

All my life, I've stowed what I loved most

safe away.

IF YOU GO AWAY

When death finds me, if there be sight
at all, let me see as the torn
coyote does, turning its head
briefly, looking not with understanding but
      recognition at where the flesh falls open around
a wound that more resembles
the marsh violet's petals, that hard-to-
detect-at-first darkening that happens—soft,
steadily—toward the flower's throat. Why not
      let go of it, I used to think, meaning that
instinct by which the body shields itself
from what threatens it unexpectedly—a fist,
the next so-called unbearable
question that's bearable after all, voilà,
      surprise . . . I know death's
an abstraction, but I prefer
a shape to things, though the shapes
are changeable. In my latest version,
      death is a young man with a habit for using
one side of his mouth to blow his hair slightly

up from his brow, while with the other half he
mutters things like *Each time I leave,*
        it's like I've left forever. Behind him,
stray cabbage moths lifting up from
the catalpa's blossoms make it seem as if
one bloom had flown free
from the others, fluttering mirror from a clutch
        of still ones. There's a kind of love that
doesn't extend itself both ways
between two people equally because it doesn't have to.

WHAT THE LOST ARE FOR

Here, before these shadows that,
in their disappearing, returning,
then falling as softly again
elsewhere, have sometimes
seemed the first and last lesson
left on the nature of power, though
they are not that, I bow my head,

I bend my knee. I hardly care,
I think, anymore who goes there,
only let me pass—however
flawed—among them, my fears
not stripped from me, but kept
hidden as, more often than not,
just beneath stamina, somewhere

grace, too, lies hidden. Nobody
speaks to me as you do. Nowhere
water-lit do the leaves pale faster.

ROCKABYE

Weeping, he seemed more naked
than when he'd been naked—more, even, than when
we'd both been. *Time to pitch your sorrifying*
someplace else, I keep meaning to say to him, and then
keep not saying it. Lightning bugs, fireflies—hasn't what
we called them made every difference. As when history
sometimes, given chance enough, in equal proportion
at once delivers
                    and shrouds meaning . . . About love: a kind
of scaffolding, I used to say. Illumination seemed
a trick meant to make us think we'd seen a thing more
clearly, before it all went black. *Why not let what's broken*
stay broken, sings the darkness, I
                                        make the darkness
sing it . . . Across the field birds fly like the storm-shook shadows
of themselves, and not like birds. Never mind. They're flying.

HIS MASTER'S VOICE

—See that's the thing you're not getting, though, the part about
honesty being at worst a bruising experience, at best
a bruisable one . . .

*

I woke regretting everything all over again, since when is that
a crime?

*

      And then woke wanting the kind of sentence whose
unfolding brings to mind a road
                    so untraveled that
indistinguishable brown birds do their dust-bath thing
right there, in the middle of it, to either side the shot
bedragglement of wild dahlias, their fake-looking posture
of half collapse, swoon of summer, the heat behaving
the way eventually the facts do with a truth more difficult
to touch than usual, that same
                         haloing out, around it, think
sea anemones when seen from above, through water, and softly waving . . .

THAT IT MIGHT SAVE,

OR DROWN THEM

I have seen how the earth erodes differently
from the way that trust does. Likewise,
I know what it means, to come to love
all over again the very mistakes I
also know, looking back, I might better have
strayed clear of. Two points make a line—but
so does one point, surely, when pulled at
once in two opposed directions: how
to turn away from what's familiar, for
example, toward what isn't

defines hope well enough, but can define,
too, despair . . . When I look around
at all the wood that's drifted ashore, been
bleached clean, and stranded, I think
to be stranded must mean giving in
to whatever forces make of strandedness
over time such smooth-to-the-hand forms
of trophy as these before me now, each one

distinctive. There's a light that can make
finding a thing look more than faintly
like falling across it—you must kneel,
make an offering. I threw my compass away
years ago. I have passed through that light.

GENTLY, THOUGH, GENTLE

Now that neglect only half excuses the field's contagion,

it's not enough to look back at the past as at a thing

to shy from, this is not

nostalgia, you must look at it,

try to, just as steadily as, for entire days, you watched

bees ferry water up from the moss-conquered

birdbath to their hive, presumably, in the chestnut's

branches, that moment-at-last in summer when

the release that fall will be

again seems possible, the way

within aggression you still want to believe

always something more tender, given a chance, will show

too, eventually, as if "flowers

first, then the fruit" were what you'd meant

all along by a clean arrangement, the door this time

closing not so slowly, your hand turning the lights down

democratically upon the heat, the night, its night song . . .

THE WEDDING

Where there's nothing but shade, ever,
he plants sea oats and ferns, lamb's ears for
the soft down that covers them, that he calls
fur. His
        "shadow garden." A grown man,
around whom the air itself, sometimes, seems
to tremble like a man trying hard not to, lest
he seem unmanly. For his own part, he says
mercy may well be the better part of conquest,
but
        Take No Prisoners has gotten him this far—
why mess with it now? Things like that; out of
nowhere. And then, as if the truth required it—
his version, anyway—whole stretches of silence,
for hours after, long enough to start dreaming up
impossible reasons for why the pines barely
move, like it's because they've
                                gone stiff with
superiority over the other trees, doomed
to leaflessness soon enough . . . *Let them strut,*

if that's strutting, he'll say, addressing
who knows what—the clouds, his hunting dogs,
as if it made
               no difference. —And this, once:
*So much of life already gets spent fucking loss
and/or getting fucked by it,* he said, looking
hard at me, *Don't you want to find happiness?*

MORE TENDERLY OVER
SOME OF US THAN OTHERS

And the wheel, as promised,
in time turning; the light Homeric now, now merely
Virgilian, predictably
            flashing off the waves that toss between
sincerity and authenticity in the storm's wake, *If they can make
no difference, why these feelings?* And the whole crew gone missing . . .

THE WAY ONE ANIMAL
TRUSTS ANOTHER

Somewhere between what it feels like, to be at
one with the sea, and to understand the sea as
mere context for the boat whose engine refuses
finally to turn over: yeah, I know the place—
stumbled into it myself, once; twice, almost. All
around and in between the two trees that
grow there, tree of compassion and—much taller—
tree of pity, its bark more bronze, the snow
            settled as if an openness of any kind meant, as well,
a woundedness that, by filling it, the snow
might heal . . . You know what I think? I think if we're
lost, you should know exactly where, by now; I've
watched you stare long and hard enough at the map
already . . . I'm beginning to think I may never
not be undecided, about all sorts of things: whether
snow really does resemble the broken laughter
            of the long abandoned when what left comes back
big-time; whether gratitude's just a haunted

space like any other. This place sounds daily
more like a theater of war, each time I listen to it—
loss, surprise, victory, being only three of the countless
fates, if you want to call them that, that we don't
so much live with, it seems, as live for now among. If as
close as we're ever likely to get, you and I, is this—this close—

A STILLNESS BETWEEN THE
HUNTING AND THE CHASE

Because there's been trouble—but when
isn't there?—this time to do with the people, after
years of forgetting, suddenly unforgetting that while
        tribute can mean acknowledgment, respect, etc., it's
also meant, historically, the price to be paid for
what was never freedom—it only looked like that—
        the king's mounted his horse. Disappointment?
If there's any inside me, he thinks, let it work
the way hunger in falcons makes the eye
        more keen. He knows enough, if not everything,
about vision being sight, vigilance a form of sometimes
looking and sometimes prayer, if attention is
        prayer, as every half century or so someone seems
eager to say again, like it's the first time . . . In the one
dream left from childhood, there's always a ship,
        just now visible; still far. But this is waking,
and this his favorite horse, whom he's never named,
that's how much he loves her, though she's

branded, sure, the way all his horses are: "Without
mystery, what chance for hope"—in Latin, on the left
flank where it catches the light, loses it, the king
      sashless and in flight, though it looks processional,
he thinks—stately, almost—as the newly fallen believe
at first there's still a plan available: they'll save themselves.

BEFORE THE LEAVES TURN BACK

Though I've shot the owl down, it hasn't stopped its trembling, so I have to still it. I cup my hand as for a shield, a sign—both— until it looks like my idea, at least, of mercy beside the one wing where I've broken it . . . A bit of brightness on the side, please, if there's some for sparing—I'm pretty sure that's how the song goes. I don't know yet that an owl's wing, when nailed to a barn's door, means protection—otherwise, I'd keep it; but that time in a life when the kind of happiness that's made in part from sorrow isn't yet the only kind: I can hear it finishing. Where are you? The only sound, for miles, is the sound of finishing.

FOR IT FELT LIKE POWER

They'd only done what all along they'd come
intending to do. So they lay untouched by regret,
after. The combined light and shadow of passing
cars stutter-shifted across the walls the way,
in summer,
                    the night moths used to, softly
sandbagging the river of dream against dream's
return . . . Listen, it's not like I don't get it about
suffering being relative—I get it. Not so much
the traces of ice on the surface of four days'
worth of rainwater in a stone urn, for example,
but how, past the ice,
                                        through the water beneath it,
you can see the leaves—sycamore—where they fell
unnoticed. Now they look suspended, like heroes
inside the myth heroes seem bent on making
from the myth of themselves; or like sunlight, in fog.

CRAFT AND VISION

Though the casting of light can't really be called—not at
least believably—in any way a property of shipwreck
once the wrecking's done with, what harm's left, now,
in saying so? As for those who would argue otherwise,
let them. Always, if it's wanted badly enough, there's
somewhere a findable veil just waiting to be lifted or pulled
slowly aside, classic revelation, a word that itself at its
root has a veil within it, somehow making the word feel
all the more like proof, as if proof meant nakedness, as if one
and the same—darkness

                    and weather; force, and sex. Every
thing I do I had to do a first time, even if I've forgotten it;
after that, I think the rest, what follows—the second time,
the last, etc.—it's all just translation, this life coming down to
the same three questions I'm told—and believe, most days—
it always has: What happened, what didn't happen, who does it
matter to? Write what you must, then walk away from it is
not the hardest thing I've ever had to learn, by any stretch,
only one of the hardest. Witness, then blindness—that's a way
of putting it. To be clear, by blindness I mean the deepest
blue possible, good cotton, not silk, the blindfold.

CROSSING

Now that, at best, we'd rowed halfway across the woods
that we mostly thought of our lives as—despite the fact
of water—accepting our position, and understanding it,
still mattered, but not like remembering what
the point had been, why we'd set out at all, from
the very start: to release something, but what? whatever
the erotic version might be of a soul we ourselves scarce

believed in? A persuasive sound to that, but if nothing else
we'd at least learned to trust sound only so far, even as
we'd had to figure out the hard way to stop giving out trust
as if trust were sex, and not what more often just gets

confused with sex . . . Above us, what sang like water was
just the wash of trees, now moving, now at rest in a wind's
disruption. A slight rustling beneath us, as of fruit unfalling
from the ground it fell to, each time we'd lift our oars
free of the waves, and steady them there, respite, shadows
in a mirror, bruises on the larger bruise of the sea's black face.

MONOMOY

Somewhere, people must still do things like fetch
water from wells in buckets, then pour it out
for those animals that, long domesticated, would
likely perish before figuring out how to get
for themselves. That dog, for example, whose
refusal to leave my side I mistook, as a child,
for loyalty—when all along it was just blind . . . What
is it about vulnerability that can make the hand
draw back, sometimes, and can sometimes seem
the catalyst for rendering the hand into sheer force,
destructive? *Don't you see how you've burnt almost*
all of it, all the tenderness, away, someone screams
to someone else, in public—and looking elsewhere,
we walk quickly past, as if even to have heard
that much might have put us at risk of whatever fate
questions like that
                    spring from. Estrangement—
like sacrifice—begins as a word at first, soon it's
the stuff of drama, cue the follow-up tears that
attend drama, then it's pretty much the difference

between waking up to a storm and waking up
inside one. Who can say how she got there—
in the ocean, I mean—but I once watched a horse
make her way back to land mid-hurricane: having
ridden, surfer-like, the very waves that at any moment
could have overwhelmed her in their crash to shore, she
shook herself, looked back once on the water's restlessness—
history's always restless—and the horse stepped free.

IF YOU WILL, I WILL

To each his own urgency. I've spent this morning clearing
best as I can the strange pornography that last night's
storms made of the trees in the yard: oak and pear branches
everywhere; of the saplings, one broken, the other in need
of retying—its roots meanwhile, where the topsoil's gotten
washed away, left exposed to a spring that, not yet done settling
in, can't be trusted. I like a wreckage I can manage myself,
the chance it offers for that particular version of power
that comes from winnowing cleanly the lost from the still
salvageable, not erasing disorder exactly, but returning
order to a fair footing, at least, beside a wilderness I wouldn't
live without. I've got this friend—I guess you could call him that—
who worries I'll never stop courting recklessness—his
word for it—as a way of compensating for or maybe making
room, where there should

                      be no room, for something torn
inside. Who can say if that's right? After a life of no signs
of it, he's found faith, and wants to know if I'm ready, finally,
to—as, again, he puts it—put my hand in the Lord's. For
the ancient Greeks—though others, too, must have thought this—

the gods were compelled most by rhythm, that's why ritual
was so important, the patterning of it, rhythm's lost
without pattern. I don't doubt that the gods—if that's
what you want to call whatever happens in this world, or
doesn't, or not as you hoped, or hoped for once it wouldn't—
seem as likely as any of us to be distracted by rhythm into
turning from one thing toward something else, but if what
comes in return is the gods' briefly full attention, though
magisterial at first, maybe—well, good luck dealing
with that. As when
                                    intimacy seems nothing more, anymore, than
a form of letting what's been simple enough become difficult,
because now less far. Or as when, looking into a mirror,
I've looked closer still, and seen the rest that I'd missed earlier:
fierce regret, with its flames for fingers, hope as the not-so-
dark holdover from the dark before . . . Despite our differences,
we agree about most things, my friend and I, or let's say it
gets harder for me, as the years go by, to know for sure
he's wrong. It's like a game between us. He says my
moods are like the images any burst of starlings makes
against an open sky, before flying away. I say either no one's
listening, this late, or else anyone is. *You've changed*, he says,
getting slowly dressed again. *You don't know me*, I say, I say back.

WILD IS THE WIND

About what's past, *Hold on when you can*, I used to say,
And when you can't, let go, as if memory were one of those
mechanical bulls, easily dismountable, should the ride
turn rough. I lived, in those days, at the forest's edge—
metaphorically, so it can sometimes seem now, though
the forest was real, as my life beside it was. I spent
much of my time listening to the sounds of random, un-
knowable things dropping or being dropped from, variously,
a middling height or a great one until, by winter, it was
just the snow falling, each time like a new, unnecessary
taxonomy or syntax for how to parse what's plain, snow
from which the occasional lost hunter would emerge
every few or so seasons, and—just once—a runaway child
whom I gave some money to and told no one about,

having promised . . . *You must keep what you've promised
very close to your heart, that way you'll never forget*
is what I've always been told. I've been told quite
a lot of things. They hover—some more unbidden than
others—in that part of the mind where mistakes and torn

wishes echo as in a room that's been newly cathedraled,
so that the echo surprises, though lately it's less the echo
itself that can still most surprise me about memory—
it's more the time it takes, going away: a mouth opening
to say *I love sex with you too it doesn't mean I wanna stop*
my life for it, for example; or just a voice, mouthless,
asking *Since when does the indifference of the body's*
stance when we're alone, unwatched, in late light, amount

to cruelty? For the metaphysical poets, the problem
with weeping for what's been lost is that tears
wash out memory and, by extension, what we'd hoped
to remember. If I refuse, increasingly, to explain, isn't
explanation, at the end of the day, what the sturdier
truths most resist? It's been my experience that
tears are useless against all the rest of it that, if I
could, I'd forget. That I keep wanting to stay should
count at least for something. I'm not done with you yet.

THE SEA, THE FOREST

Like an argument against keeping the more unshakable varieties of woundedness inside, where such things maybe best belong, he opened his eyes in the dark. *Did you hear that*, he asked . . . I became, all over again, briefly silver, as in what the leaves mean, beneath, I could hear what sounded like waves at first, then like mistakes when, having gathered momentum, they crash wave-like against the shore of everything that a life has stood for. —*What*, I said.

NOTES AND ACKNOWLEDGMENTS

With many thanks to the editors of the following journals, wherein these poems first appeared, sometimes in different form:

Academy of American Poets/Poem-a-Day: "Swimming," "The Way One Animal Trusts Another"

Bear Review: "If You Will, I Will"

Callaloo: "Gently, Though, Gentle" (as "The Dark No Softer Than It Was Before"), "More Tenderly Over Some of Us Than Others" (as "Let's Get Lost"), "Rockabye," "The Wedding"

The Cincinnati Review: "The Distance and the Spoils," "Not the Waves as They Make Their Way Forward"

Green Mountains Review: "The Dark No Softer Than It Was Before" (as "Deciduous")

Kenyon Review: "Black and Copper in a Crush of Flowers," "His Master's Voice," "If You Go Away"

The Manchester Review (UK): "Crossing," "From a Bonfire," "Gold Leaf"

The Nation: "That It Might Save, or Drown Them"

Phantom Limb: "Courtship"

Plume: "Revolver"

Poet Lore: "And Love You Too"

Poetry: "Brothers in Arms," "Monomoy," "Musculature," "Stray,"
  "Wild Is the Wind"
Poetry Northwest: "Before the Leaves Turn Back"
Revolver: "Givingly"
Sugar House Review: "Meditation: On Being a Mystery to Oneself,"
  "The Sea, the Forest"
T Magazine/The New York Times: "What I See Is the Light Falling All
  Around Us"
32 Poems: "A Stillness Between the Hunting and the Chase"

*

"Gold Leaf" is for Tom Knechtel.

"Several Birds in Hand but the Rest Go Free" originally appeared in *And Across Our Faces*, a limited-edition chapbook published by Tim Geiger at Aureole Press, University of Toledo, Ohio, 2015. "Courtship," "The Sea, the Forest," and "Givingly" were reprinted in the same chapbook.

"Rockabye" also appeared in *The Best American Poetry 2017*, edited by Natasha Trethewey and David Lehman, Scribner, New York, 2017.

"A Stillness Between the Hunting and the Chase": The motto "Without mystery, what chance for hope" is a variation of part of a sentence in Ali Smith's *How to Be Both*, Anchor Books, New York, 2015. It's from that book, as well, that I learned of the Renaissance correlation between hunger and vision in the training of falcons.

"For It Felt Like Power" was first published as a limited-edition broadside by Counterproof Press in the Art & Art History Department, School of Fine Arts, at the University of Connecticut in conjunction with my visit as the Wallace Stevens Poet, March 2016.

"Craft and Vision": The opening is in response to George Oppen's phrase "the bright light of shipwreck," from section 9 of *Of Being Numerous*; "What happened, what didn't happen, who does it matter to" is from *Reputations* by Juan Gabriel Vásquez, Riverhead Books, New York, 2016.

The italicized line in "Monomoy" is a variation on a sentence in Iris Murdoch's *The Sea, the Sea*, Penguin Books, New York, 1980.

"Wild Is the Wind": Thank you to Annalise Duerden, whose dissertation, "Mortal Verse: Memory in Early Modern Poetry of Love, Grief, and Devotion," directed me to the relationship between tears and memory in the work of Donne and his contemporaries.